LITTL[E]

Dinosaurs

Christopher Maynard

Kingfisher Books

Contents

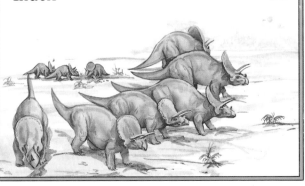

Long, long ago...

M illions and millions of years ago lots of very strange-looking monsters roamed the Earth. Dinosaurs were probably not all that intelligent. Yet many of them were so big and powerful they were able to settle in almost every part of the world. Then, after 150 million years of great success, these huge beasts suddenly vanished from the face of the Earth. To this day, nobody is really sure why they died out so quickly after so many years.

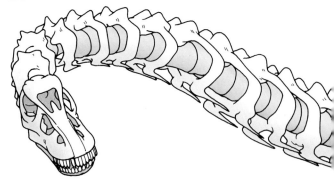

D inosaurs disappeared millions of years before there were any people on Earth. Yet we have learnt a lot about them from the fossils that scientists have discovered.

Sometimes a dinosaur's body became covered by mud and sand soon after it died. Its body slowly rotted away, but the bones that made up its skeleton were protected. Over the years, these bones became rock-hard fossils.

Scientists who dig up fossils may piece together an entire skeleton, yet they cannot really know what the skin or muscles of the animal looked like.

Putting together a fossil skeleton is like solving a giant jigsaw puzzle, only harder. You can be sure there will always be some missing bits.

Big and small

Dinosaurs came in all shapes and sizes. But not all of them lived at the same time, or in the same part of the world. A few stood as tall as buildings. Others were no bigger than a chicken.

In between, there were light-weight dinosaurs that ran nimbly on two hind legs and heavyweights that plodded about on all fours.

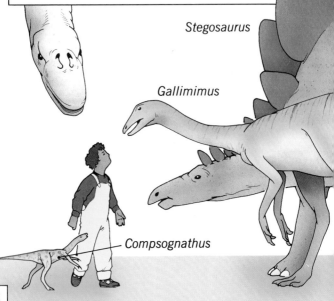

Stegosaurus

Gallimimus

Compsognathus

Apatosaurus

Parasaurolophus

Triceratops

Euoplocephalus

Back in time

T he world was very different back then. The weather was warm all year round and forests of strange trees and giant ferns, as well as many other unfamiliar plants, covered the land.

Although the name dinosaur means 'terrible lizard', most of the dinosaurs were peaceful plant-eaters.

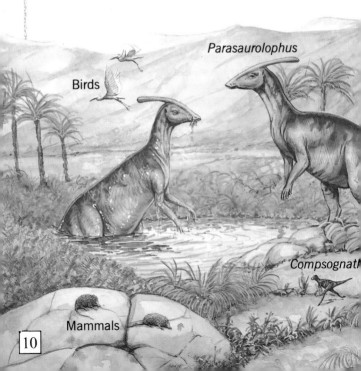

Birds

Parasaurolophus

Compsognath

Mammals

The dinosaurs shared their world with many kinds of other animals too. The first birds soared alongside giant flying reptiles. Small lizards basked on sunny rocks. While tiny furred mammals, no bigger than rats, scurried about in the undergrowth.

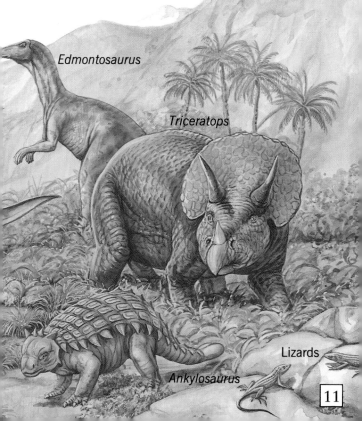

Edmontosaurus

Triceratops

Ankylosaurus

Lizards

The giants

The biggest dinosaurs of all were the sauropods, or 'lizard feet'. However their feet would be the last part you would notice. The main thing about them was their incredible size.

One of the biggest of the sauropods was *Brachiosaurus*. It had legs like tree trunks, and the front legs were longer than those at the back. Its long neck helped it to browse in tree tops, like a giraffe. It was so tall it could have peered over a five-storey building.

From the tip of its tail to the end of its small nose, *Brachiosaurus* was nearly as long as three buses.

DINOSAUR HEAVYWEIGHTS

One *Brachiosaurus* would have weighed more than eight elephants.

13

Build a Brachiosaurus

A simple model of a dinosaur is quite easy to make. All you need is tracing paper, thick card, a pair of scissors and brightly coloured paints.

Trace the three shapes shown here on to the thick card and cut out each of them carefully. Then cut the slot spaces. Paint both sides of the shapes. Then slot the shapes together as shown on the opposite page.

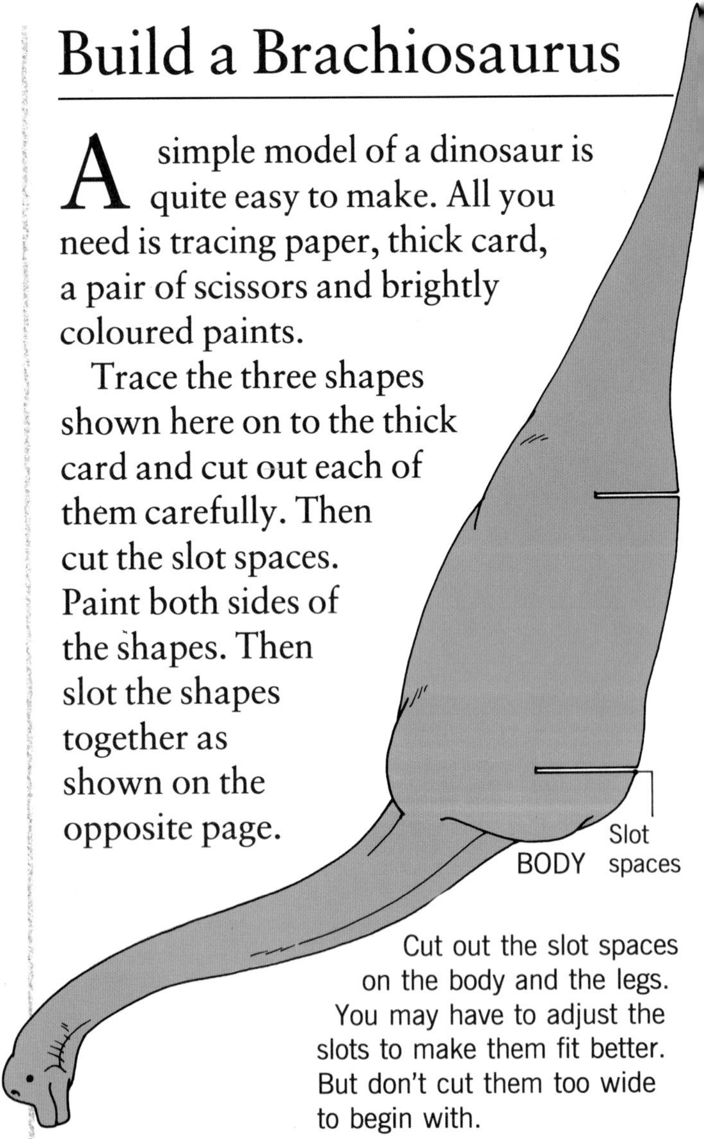

BODY

Slot spaces

Cut out the slot spaces on the body and the legs. You may have to adjust the slots to make them fit better. But don't cut them too wide to begin with.

14

Slot spaces

FRONT LEGS

BACK LEGS

Slot the pieces together once the paint has dried. Make sure the long legs go at the front.

No one knows for sure what colour dinosaurs were. If you find grey or green a bit boring, try painting them other colours.

Timid plant-eaters

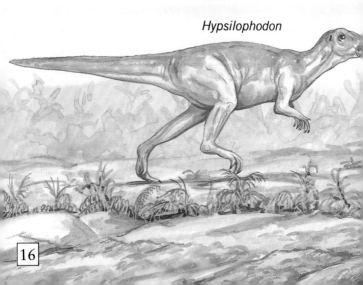

T he 'bird-footed' dinosaurs, or ornithopods, were timid planteating creatures. Instead of front teeth most had beaks, and instead of claws they had little nails or hooves.

They relied on keen eyesight to keep them out of danger. Some also stayed together in herds for greater protection from the big meat-eaters. If a look-out called a warning, all the animals in the herd would swiftly sprint to safety on their long, strong hind legs.

Hypsilophodon

Some types of ornitho-pods had a hollow crest on their head, which they may have used like a hooter. These are called the hadrosaurs, or 'big lizards'.

Other ornithopods, such as *Hypsilophodon*, were smaller but could run faster.

Parasaurolophus (a hadrosaur)

Corythosaurus (a hadrosaur)

17

Armour plated

A rmoured plant-eaters didn't need to run as fast as the bird-footed dinosaurs. These heavy beasts could stand their ground and put up a good defence if they were attacked.

Some had bony plates along their back. Others had a shield of armour from head to tail. A few also had sharp horns or clubbed tails.

Stegosaurus had a tiny brain about the size of a walnut, but it also had a spiked tail to defend itself with.

Euoplocephalus, or 'well-armoured head', was built like a tank. It was short and heavy, and covered from head to tail in an armour of bony plates. The tip of the tail ended in a heavy bony club, which it could swing at its attackers.

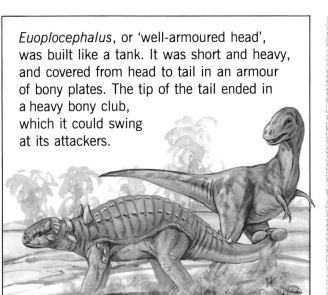

Triceratops looked a little like a rhinoceros, but was bigger and heavier. It lived in herds and the adults may have guarded their young by forming a circle with their horns facing out.

Small and deadly

S ome of the fiercest dinosaurs were not really all that big. One of these was 'bird robber' (*Ornitholestes*). It was not much taller than an average person, but it darted about fast enough to hunt down small lizards and birds.

'Terrible claw' (*Deinonychus*) was a good name for a deadly dinosaur that was able to kill animals many times bigger than itself. It had two huge curved claws with which to tear its victims apart.

Ornitholestes

Deinonychus hunted in packs.
It had a huge claw on each
hind foot which it used
to slash at its prey.

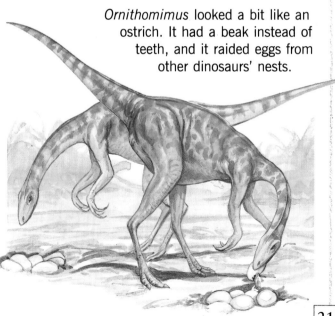

Ornithomimus looked a bit like an
ostrich. It had a beak instead of
teeth, and it raided eggs from
other dinosaurs' nests.

Fierce beasts

The 'tyrant lizard' (*Tyrannosaurus*) was the most fearsome killer of all the dinosaurs. It was a giant – as heavy as an elephant and as tall as a giraffe. An adult human would have reached no higher than its knees.

It had jaws wide enough to swallow a person whole. Its teeth would have been like rows of sharp kitchen knives.

Tyrannosaurus

DRAW A TYRANNOSAURUS

Follow each of the steps shown here.

① ② ③ ④ ⑤ ⑥

23

Dinosaur babies

F ossils of nests and eggs found by scientists tell us a lot about the way dinosaur mothers cared for their newborn young. Scientists think that dinosaurs laid eggs, just like turtles, crocodiles and other reptiles do today. *Protoceratops* left her eggs in a shallow nest of sand, where the Sun's heat could keep them warm.

Baby dinosaurs were very small and always at risk from hungry hunters. They had to grow very quickly in order to survive if they were left unprotected.

△The 'good mother lizard' (*Maiasaura*) stayed close to her babies to protect them until they could look after themselves.

A newly-hatched *Protoceratops* would have been small enough to hold in your hand. But it soon grew to be six times as long.

Protoceratops covered her eggs with sand

Skies and seas

W hile the dinosaurs were the biggest beasts on land, other creatures ruled the seas and the skies.

There were 'fish lizards' (ichthyosaurs) and 'ribbon lizards' (plesiosaurs) in the oceans. They all had sharp teeth with which to catch their prey.

In the air, pterosaurs flapped and glided about on wings of leathery skin. One of these, *Pteranodon*, had wings so long they could spread over a house.

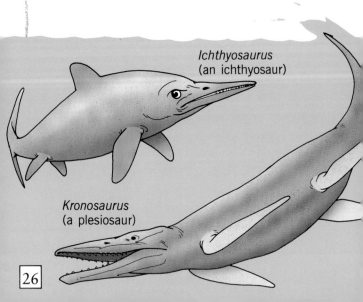

Ichthyosaurus
(an ichthyosaur)

Kronosaurus
(a plesiosaur)

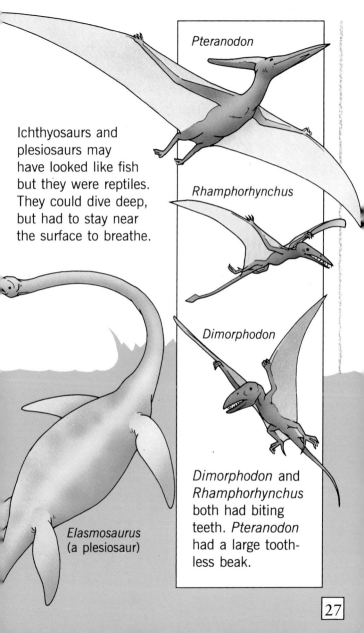

Pteranodon

Ichthyosaurs and plesiosaurs may have looked like fish but they were reptiles. They could dive deep, but had to stay near the surface to breathe.

Rhamphorhynchus

Dimorphodon

Elasmosaurus (a plesiosaur)

Dimorphodon and *Rhamphorhynchus* both had biting teeth. *Pteranodon* had a large tooth-less beak.

27

The last dinosaurs

V ery suddenly, around 65 million years ago, the dinosaurs all died out. Nobody knows why. It is possible that the weather became too cold for them. Or perhaps a terrible disease struck them down.

Some scientists think a comet, a ball of rock from Space, may have smashed into Earth so hard that clouds of dust surrounded the planet for many years.

Clouds of dust from a colliding comet may have blocked out the Sun's light and cooled the Earth so much that the dinosaurs couldn't survive. The tiny lizards and mammals had better luck.

Alamosaurus

Mammals

Why not make your own dinosaur scrapbook? See how many different dinosaurs you can find for each letter of the alphabet. Make a note of where each one lived and list all of its special features.

Tyrannosaurus

Lizard

Index